George Engelmann

George Engelmann and John Torrey Correspondence,

1841-1862

George Engelmann

George Engelmann and John Torrey Correspondence, 1841-1862

ISBN/EAN: 9783337321116

Printed in Europe, USA, Canada, Australia, Japan

Cover: Foto ©ninafisch / pixelio.de

P. Vaé Roy Esq

Dear Sir

You will find a number of sets of the Plants you desire at Messrs Wiley & Putnam's, booksellers of your city, who sell them in commission. By applying to them you will save yourself time and expense of transportation from here.

A descriptive Catalogue of these plants has been published in the January Nro of Silliman's Journal, if Extra copies of it should not be in the hands of Messrs W & P. you can undoubtedly obtain them in a few weeks, as they ought to be added to the sets

Respectfully yours

St Louis Mo Jan 22 1844

George Engelmann

Recd. July 19

St Louis July 8th 1844

Dear Sir

I am glad, you received the small parcel of plants sent to you, nearly a year ago! In September last I sent a box containing different parcels of plants to Mssrs Wiley & Putnam; the box contained also letters, dated August 26th for you and others. Some of the parcels have come to their destination soon, others only in the last months, and some not even yet, so far as I know — Your parcel was directed to Carey & Co. 90. Pinestreet N. York —

I am very grateful for the small, though quite sufficient specimen of Cusc. umbellata. As it is of importance for our flora, I will try to get a few flowers of Humboldt's specimen from Berlin or Paris, to be able to compare them. — At present I have only what Choisy copies from Kunth - he not having seen the plant himself. His description is very incomplete but agrees as far as it goes with Dr James' Plant, except that in this the lobes of the corolla appear not to be reflexed but erect or somewhat open and the filaments are not linear but subulate from a broad base; size of flower, length of pedicels etc. agree —

Dr James' plant is nearly related with my C. Polygonorum and C. pentagona, also somewhat with C. americana (the westindian). They are distinguished by the finer texture of the flower, principally the corolla also the capsule and by the depressed ovary and capsule, without any thing like a stylopodium. Some have the dry corolla covering the capsule (C. americ. from the Westindies, C. Cephalanthi (Missouri, and C. cuspidata, Texas)

In others the dry corolla remains at base of the capsule as in your plant, as I believe, not having seen a capsule (Can you ascertain it from actual observation? I judge from the shape of the corolla) & my C. Polygonorum and C. pentagona. C. californica also probably belongs here. — All the other North American species known to me (except C. verrucosa) have a stylopodium, and a more solid, coriaceous texture of all parts of the flower. — Your plant is distinguished from C. Polyg. & C. pentag. by the few flowered corymbs and long pedicels; also from C. Pol. by the 5 parted flowers, their small size, the well developped scaly appendages and the filiform styles; from C. pentag. by the acute calyx lobes, the longer filaments, the different shape of corolla etc.

What species of Cuscuta have you in New York? I know only C. Gronovii (my vulgivaga) and C. Saururi (a bad name) in western New York, and the (undoubtedly imported) C. Epilinum. — C. G. & C. S. you may perhaps consider identical and I think your suggestion as to the difficulty to ascertain the limits of some of my species, must refer to these two plants. Still I think I can always distinguish them well, and have not found yet any intermediate forms here, where they are both common. C. S. I have also received from Kentucky abundantly. — I am sorry that no copy of the Annals of the N.Y. Lyceum is within my reach, so I can not ascertain what you have said about C. umbellata; — it is certainly different from any of mine. —

Rafinesque's two plants are perhaps C. glomerata Choisy (my Lepidanche); [illegible] the stemless state of the plant in flowering, sessile flowers, capitate dense whorls in one and large amplexicaul glomerations in the other, the long styles in both appear to indicate it; also the names paradoxa & acaulis; but I have seen no Cuscuta yet without appendages! and am anxious to see one or two South-american ones described as destitute of them; — then

C. parad. is said to have a 5 parted flower and 4 lobes of the corolla and 4 stamina! C. acaulis is said to have a corolla campanulate and urceolate! None of ours flowers in June. Rafin. describes another species in Spreng. neue Entdeck. 1. p. 145 according to Choisy: C. aphylla, floribus sessilibus glomeratis 4-fidis stigmatibus capitatis. Hab. super compositis ad Wabash: I can not ascertain that! — —

I will assist you as well as I can in your Monogr. of the Asclep., and with so much greater pleasure, as I take a great interest in that tribe and have already made drawings of the flowers of different species here. We have here Asclepias tuberosa, incarnata, purpurascens.? syriaca verticillata, obtusifolia amplexicaulis Acerates longifolia and viridiflora, Enslenia albida. Some other species grow some distance from here, in the leadbearing hills of the South West. — If you want drawings of any of them, you will oblige me by naming the species, and it would be best to give me a rough sketch of some species, you have already drawn so that I can see how you wish to have it executed. Drawings of parts of Acerates viridiflora longifolia lanceolata and a new? species which I have called A. Geyeri (collected by Geyer for Fremont on the Desmoines River) I have already made, also of Asclepias purpurascens, Podostigma? and one or two others from dried specimens. — A. Geyeri is remarkable for its long cylindrical root 1/2 to 3/4 inch thick. —

Dr Wunderly has been warmly recommended to me by my friend A Braun in Carlsruhe, and I have some fine plants collected by him in the South of France. His scheme to go to the far west is impracticable, at least this season. —

You have heard of the unheard of inundations, which have also prevented me from a trip to the South west of our state. — The travellers in the west have suffered much by then; Fremont if not detained in the Mountains was probably kept back by the floods. We know nothing yet from him, except that notice from California

I can try to get drawings of Asclep. from Mr Lindheimer in Texas, who is a very fair draftsman, if you will indicate the Species etc. — He has sent me nothing yet, which is not also in the southern States. —

I have not got any specimens or fragments yet from Dr Gray from your herbarium, so far as I recollect; some 3 years ago he sent me some Cuscutineae from his own. But I shall ask him for them. —

I remain, very respectfully
yours
G Engelmann

Prof. J. Torrey
Princeton

Prof John Torrey
Princeton
New Jersey

St Louis Dec. 12th 1844

Dear Sir

Your letter of August 2d reached me in due time, but it found me in a season of sickliness, when professional business occupied every moment and left me no leisure for botanical studies. So it was left unanswered for a while, and nothing was done in regard to Asclepiadeae. I find that we have only two here, not included in your list of New Jersey plants of this family: Acerates longifolia and Enslenia albida; perhaps also Asclepias amplexicaulis, but this last I could not find again since some years. — In the Southern parts of the State we have some more, some species of Gonolobus, and the large flowered Acerates paniculata Dcne (is that an Acerates? I doubt it if my plant is really Decaisne's), on the northern state line, or perhaps rather in Iowa we have a species of Acerates which I think is undescribed by Decaisne, but must be near his A. angustifolia it was collected by Mr Geyer 1841 when he was on the Desmoines River in company of Lieut. Fremont; I obtained from him a poor specimen, and a few others came with Mr F.'s collections to Washington, I named it then after its discoverer A. Geyeri

Acerates, radice cylindrica tuberosa, caule erecto simplici, foliis alternis linearibus, margine scabris umbellis pedunculatis, pedunculis pedicellis paulo brevioribus, cucullis gynostegium aequantibus, apice 3 dentatis. Sinu intermedio brevissimo...

Amongst the Texas plants, received a few months ago was also a species of Asclepias (Otaria) which is not described by Decaisne, and is therefore probably not been collected by Berlandier or Drummond. It appears to be nearest to A. longicorne Benth. I have not had time yet to examine it more carefully. Amongst the Texas plants sent to Dr Gray a few weeks ago is also a complete specimen of this species for you, with fruit etc; it has a tuberous root. There are also several species of Gonolobus not yet examined by me. —

You will do me a favour by making a rough sketch with the pen in your next letter ~~of some~~ a copy of some one of your drawings of ~~some~~ a species, with all the details, in short a rough copy of one plate, so that I can see the size, and the manner of exhibiting the different parts of the flower etc, and that I can make my drawings next season accordingly. I will promise you Acerates longifolia & Enslenia at all events, if I live and have my health.

Fremont writes me that you have seen his plants, and that they are in a miserable condition. He promised me duplicates, but I suppose there are none to spare. I have got letters from Geyer from Fort Colville, Oregon from April last; he will not send any plants here, but take them to England. — Mr Lüders had collected nothing last spring, when Fremont saw him on the Columbia, he had lost every thing in the river. I have no further news from him. Lindheimer is collecting in the west of Texas, and a large box must be on the Mississippi now from him, if not lost in some snagged steamboat.

If you will name those plants of Lindheimer, which you wish especially I will try to procure them for you just give me the numbers if you can get at them. Dr Gray must have now near 300 numbers, and I hope to get a hundred more in the next box. As Mr Lind. does not make a general collection, I think plants from other parts than Texas would at present be of no interest to him.

Of Rumices I know nothing. I have long ago however distributed an apparently new species allied to R. acetosella, also dioicous, growing here, and I find also in Arkansas & Texas. I had named it R. angustifolius (near R. angustissimus Ledebour from Siberia) if it should not be known to you, I will send you specimens.

Amaranthaceae & Chenopodiaceae I have not studied principally because I have no work, which I could use. The same is the case with the interesting families of Gramineae & Cyperaceae. A want of books has always deterred me from attacking the numerous material in my hand. I shall be much obliged to you for your monograph so kindly offered, and it shall be an incentive to study the Cyperaceae next season.

Your offer of specimens and books to study one or the other family is very kind, and I shall apply to you, whenever I should be in want of them. Meanwhile receive my heartfelt thanks

very truly yours

George Engelmann

Prof John Torrey M.D.
30 McDougal street
New York

My dear Sir

I am much obliged to you for offering me an opportunity to get acquainted with so zealous naturalists as your young friends appear to be. They staid here longer than they anticipated, and I had an opportunity to see them often. we also made a few botanical excursions together, and collected the few early rarities of these parts. You will probably have learnt from them that they intend to extent their trip to the shores of the pacific and to California. If their luck is equal to their zeal and their confidence, they will bring back rich treasures.

My best thanks also for the interesting parcel of pamphlets etc, of which the most valuable for me is your Cyperaceae; I have had no proper means before this to study this interesting and difficult order. I am glad that you also have sanctioned the use of the minute and often microscopic characters; I find them often of much more use than those commonly used. So with the Euphorbiae stipulatae, which I have studied lately; they are beautifully distinguished by their seeds! What is E. maculata L.? Some take it as a variety of E. hypericifolia, others name your E. depressa (= E. thymifolia of many authors) so; but Linnaeus calls it an assurgent plant. E. hypericifolia is the only one known to me with black seeds in that section. All those with serrated leaves in this section have rugose or otherwise uneven seeds, and those with entire leaves (as E polygonifolia etc) have smooth seeds! I know only one exception, a plant from the foot of the R. Mts which I have called deltoidea, it has entire leaves and rugose seeds.

I know nothing new about Cuscutae, and have learnt nothing yet about C. umbellata from Berlin, where specimens must be preserved.

My Asclepias Lindheimeri (perhaps too near A longicornu) of which I have sent you specimens by Dr Gray, is flourishing finely with me, and if it should bloom well, I shall take a drawing of it for you. Have I told you of an Asclepias which grows in this neighborhood, though very rare, near A amplexicaulis, but well distinguished? a larger plant, with larger flowers, the corona much longer than the columella etc. —

I have also six Cactus from Texas growing, of which three or four will bloom this summer, some apparently undescribed.

I have put aside for you all the texan plants you desired, except the Aristolochia, of which there were only a few specimens, which I could not retain from the regular subscribers. I shall send them by private hand in a day or two. Please consider them as a present from Mr Lindheimer. — If you could give me always a list of those texan plants among Lindheimers collections, which you desire for yourself before the distribution of the plants into sets, I can most always lay aside a specimen for you.

I forgot to thank you for the few bits of Californian plants; from that remote region every thing is most interesting. You can have no idea how near we here consider ourselves now to Oregon & California; we mentally travel with those thousands of emigrants, and begin to think the Rocky Mts not much farther off than the Alleghanies. The interest we take in the country gives a new value to its natural productions!

I shall request my friend, Mr Plump, who takes the parcel with him, to leave it at Wiley & Putnams.

Pity that Fremont is so selfish or narrow minded or the department so niggardly not to send any naturalists out with him. What an opportunity and what a field! — F. is expected here every day.

Very respectfully
yours

George Engelmann

Prof John Torrey

Princeton

N. Jersey

Prof. J. Torrey

Dear Sir

Some time ago I sent you by Mr. LeConte the only drawing I could make this summer for you, Acerates longifolia. Enslenia I had collected, but found in this very sickly season no leisure to figure. The new Asclepias, similar to A. amplexicaulis, which I had called A. glaberrima I could not find; the large plain of the American bottom, a bottomland of the Mississippi opposite St Louis, where it has been collected by me near 12 years ago had been overflowed last year, and hundreds of Acres of the lower parts are now there covered with a most luxuriant growth of Iva ciliata, which kills every thing else. other parts are under cultivation, so that it will be difficult to discover this interesting plant again. At the time I collected it, I was struck with it as being one of the latest species of the genus in flower.

I hope you have safely received the Texas plants sent to you some time in April or May.

I have a few days ago had the pleasure to look through Capt Fremonts Collection made in June & July; I understand Dr McDowell is to deliver it to you. — Among the plants of the families described in your flora, I have been most interested in your Cucumis perennis, which Dr McD informs me is common on the upper Arkansas, a new Dysodia and a large and probably new Grindelia with a copious pappus. There are 4 species (all described?)

Your most acceptable present, the Cyperaceae, has had the good effect of inducing me to study this so far by me neglected family, and I have been lucky enough to find two species of Cyperus, not described by you; and also abundantly your C. acuminatus.

We have here C. diandrus (rare.) C. diandrus var. Castaneus, C. Michauxianus C. strigosus. (also a var. with large leafy involucre, common) C. repens, C. filiculmis C. inflexus, C. acuminatus, C. ovularis, C. erythrorhizos. —

C. ovularis, C. Baldw. C. tetragonus and a fourth one from here included in paper No 1. belong evidently to one group, with 4 angular spikes, the last is the loosest and with most flowers in the spike, largest nuts etc; rhizoma tuberous and creeping, in sandy soil.

C. Michauxianus and my new one No 2 also belong together in the structure of the spikelet; articulated fragile rhachis etc; nut included entire in the interior scales in mine, only lower part in C. Mich. The new one ought to be called tenuiflorus or tenuispicus. I have found it on the muddy banks of a sluggish stream with C. Mich & C. erythrorhizos; all three annuals! C. Mich. & C. eryth. grow every where together on the banks of the Mississippi here and frequently many depressed stems, 3–6 inches long from the same base; they are rarely tall & erect. No 3 is a variety of C. strigosus? not the same, but spikes & scales different; found with very large compact umbells and very small, loose ones; might be your

I find here with the common form of Trichelostylis autumnalis with base of the style persistent ! No 4

Scirpus debilis ? spikes elongated, not deeply rugose, no setae No 5.

Scirpus lacustris, distinct from the European plant, styles two, not three, nut not half as large.

Our Scirpus pungens does not appear to be the same as Sc. triquetrus which I have collected on the banks of the Rhine, which has an effuse panicle etc.

Asclepias Lindheimeri has been thriving well with me, but the flowerbuds always fell off before coming to perfection. I shall send a tuber to Dr Gray, perhaps he will succeed better.

I have letters from Mr Lindheimer till August. He appears to have found many new things. He is botanizing west of the Guadaloupe river, not far from San Antonio.

By the next opportunity I shall send you specimens of these Cyperaceae and a few other plants, that might interest you.

Very respectfully
yours
George Engelmann

ST. LOUIS
OCT
27
MO.

10

Prof J. Torrey

Princeton

New Jersey

St. Louis, August 1st 1847

My dear Sir

Your letter dated May 27th etc was received few days ago, and I was glad to see from it, that the different things sent to you have all arrived safely.

Lindheimer is doing well in the western part of Tex. near the southern confluences of the Colorado, where the mountainous region of the cretaceous formation becomes varied by granitic hills, and where undoubtedly the vegetation is also much diversified. His collections of 1845 & 46 are now in my hands.

Set of them in the hands of Prof Gray, and if I understood him rightly he was to communicate the Asclepiadeae to you; I have examined that family and made drawings of the flowers in these parts and find many new things amongst them e.g. a [illegible], a [illegible] & others, a new Anantherix (or two) and certainly that ~~[illegible]~~ against Decaisne's opinion this the Mexicans for 5 or 6 months in the interior of the State of Chihuahua but had been liberated by the glorious battle of Sacramento. — A few weeks afterwards a large box arrived here direct from Chihuahua with minerals, plants, living Cacti, seeds and heaven knows what else! Unfortunately the box he sent from Santa Fe last year never came here — but this containing his collections from Santa Fe to Paso and Chihuahua was in fine order — the plants superb, most of the Cacti living — and now finely growing with me. — Five weeks ago he came himself as surgeon to Col. Doniphan's Missouri Troops. On the way from Chihuahua to Saltillo & Matamoros, he has also made many collections, which owing to the rapidity of the march, the arduous duties of the surgeon and the rainy season, were not as fine and interesting as the ~~last~~ former.

Dr Wislizenus has given abundant proof of his ability & energy and intends to go again west (and south) if he can get an appointment as surgeon, as he has spent his means in the last trip. — He is one of our best surgeons ...

to a number of unfortunate sick and crippled volunteers. He is a man of sufficiently acquainted with astronomy, has had the good fortune to carry safely an excellent Barometer all the way with him & back, making constant use of it — also other instruments — and is altogether the best man that could be sent out by Mr. Marcy — He and some of his friends have already applied to him, but if you would put your weight in the balance too you might do him good service.

Lindheimer is alive, & I am [illegible] not but April here have not yet [illegible]

I have got some collections from Monterey & Saltillo but nothing else from Mexico yet. —

I frequently wish to be nearer you & Gray, and the large collections & libraries — but I think my situation here is also good in the centre of western life & enterprise other private Coll. also fragments of the Paris & Berlin herbaria — and must work them out. I must establish a living Cactus collection, increasing it by new ones — those of Fendler as soon as they arrive, those of Wislizenus — must also be added;

I have lately paid much attention to Alsinaceae and should like to work this small order out by the time you come to it; I establish Richardsonia, I strongly suspect, that some european Alsineae (A. [illegible] e.g.) belong to it, and counts 3 species that grow here. —

Another family in which I take a great interest are the Cacti — and I am cultivating now probably 30 species of Texas, N. Mexico & U.S. Of course I can not trouble myself with the cultivation of more southern plants but I should like to get a complete collection of those near us — which for the most part are now quite unknown to gardening botanists. In addition I have now also Nuttall's Mamillaria vivipara (from the upper Missouri?) — I shall cultivate it, to ascertain to which it belongs to. — Do you know his Cactus ferox? "joints very large, fruit as large as a hens egg" — I have one from above, which has small joints (3 inches long) and small spiny fruits, but may be the ferox (or C. missouriensis?)

If you can help me to increase my Coll. of Cactus from the country of the Rio Grande, Chihuahua, N. Mexico, Oregon or California, I should be much obliged to you.

Dr. Wisl. has also sent a Prospectus [illegible] your [illegible] moderate but very distinct.

[illegible] glad that the plants of the Exploring Expedit. have finally come into your hands. — I shall

distinct — did he says also under the [illegible] species,
pag 453 C. babylonica Kurdistan Berg (mountain) Gen. Kotschy
— Is that your plant — as you say from the mountains
of Kurdistan; if so — Choisy is wrong, for yours and
mine are absolutely identical — — I have never
received an answer from Berlin, and don't know
whether I shall be able to compare Kunth's Cuscutae
in relation to your C. umbellata. Fremont's plant
from the same region 1844, is my C. neuropetala, which
I have also from Florida. Hooker has sent me all
his Cuscutae and promises to intercede for me
in Berlin. I ought to be able to compare Kunth's
authentic specimens, as the descriptions do not go
a great length to identify [illegible] Choisy's are

rof John Torrey

Princeton

N Jersey

My dear Sir,

Your letter of Aug 20th is more than a month [in] my hands — it would have been answered long ago if that month was not just the most busy for a medical practitioner in our region.

I am waited in vain for those drawings of Cacti — they have not come to hand — but Mr Lindheimer sent me seeds of 3 Cacti collected west[?] from Santa Fe[?] I have got new species again, and almost every [illegible] brings any thing from there brings also new species. The northern Cacti are almost unknown. Have I told you that I have now also a specimen of what must be Nuttall's Mammillaria simplex from the upper Missouri — very near my Texan M. similis.

Mr Fendler has just returned from Santa Fe with rich collections — want of means — failure of others furnishing means — have driven him back. — He, Wislizenus and Gregg have sent many Asclepiadeae — which appear very interesting. —

Dr Wislizenus has heard nothing yet from Washington but as the war appears now to continue, I hope he will have an appointment suitable to his enterprise next spring. I was pleased to see Dr Halsted's name honorably mentioned in Gen. Shields report of the battles before Mexico

Do you know, what Mr Gambel, the ornithologist from Philadelphia has done in New Mexico etc. in regard to Botany? What has become of his collection? He collected so far as I know from Nuttall.

My little Echinodorus sent to you one or two years ago is very distinct from your Alisma Geyeri, which is a true Alisma has also 9 stamens, very slender flowers and simple umbell etc. Echinodorus I think ought to comprise all Alismae with a globose head of carpells; Alisma has them verticillate; E. has mostly more than 6 stamens, though the European A. ranunculoides, ranunculoides by nature appear to belong here also; carpells ribbed

A. has 6 stamens, carpells verticillate, compressed-1-2 costate on the back, smooth on the sides, style persistent but blunt, ventral, in E pointed and rather more terminal.

Najas & Caulinia are as far entirely unknown to me, and I have not had occasion to examine them; I am much obliged to you however for your interesting communication, and shall try to study ours next spring. —

Anxious to hear about the Cuscutae of the exploring expedition — send me, if you can, fragments of all the species known or new — they will be important to me. — I had formerly applied to Mr Rich but was refused.

Truly yours

G. Engelmann

My dear Doctor

allow me to introduce to your acquaintance my friend Dr A. Wislizenus, who is already known to you by former letters from me as the explorer of the natural history of New Mexico and Chihuahua. Though he is no botanist or chemist in the strict sense of the word, still he is an accurate observer, and will be able to give you much interesting information about the botanical and mineralogical riches of the countries traversed by him.

Any favor extended to him will be gratefully acknowledged by

your friend and servt

George Engelmann

Prof John Torrey
Princeton NJ.

Prof John Torrey

Princeton

NJ

or New York

to introduce

Dr A. Wislizenus

yesterday I received your kind communication & am [illegible] much obliged to you for the interest you take in my pursuits as regards botany, and for your efforts to collect for me material, which would be valuable to me. As regards Cacti I have no doubt the largest collection of the northern forms of Cacti, that exists anywhere and am doing all I can to complete it. From Geyer's notes [in] Hooker's Journal I see, that some undescribed and to me unknown species must exist on the upper Platte & Missouri; I have got three forms from there last year: Mam. vivipara, Mam. simplex Nutt (non [illegible]) and an Opuntia which I would take for O. missouriensis if it had not small dry spiny fruit nothing like the [illegible] hens egg size. I hope to see [illegible] this coming season. — A few days ago I got amongst a few other species from Prince Salm (in Germany) a O. missouriensis! it has never flowered in Europe! — O. fragilis I have not been able yet to obtain, but shall get it probably from the same source! Dr Wislizenus has supplied me with the largest variety, and also the [illegible].

In my botanical appendix to Dr Wis.' report you will find some investigation in the generic distribution of Cacteae and [find] remarkable characters in the seeds which appear and often conspicuously, than the books will admit. But you will see all the results of my studies on this family in a few weeks in Dr W's Report. —

In Cuscutae I have done nothing lately. Dr W. has not collected any; but Fendler has brought your C. umbellata in fine specimens from Santa Fe!

I should have liked to submit my paper on Dr W's plants to you or to Dr Torrey, but every thing was so much hurried that I had not finished it, before the Dr left here. I have no doubt that many of my new things are not new to other botanists! But having compared Fremont's Report, I was aware of the proximity of Wislizenia and Oxystylis, but considered them distinct on account of the long stipe of the ovary and other characters mentioned by me; but that may not be sufficient to distinguish them — Another new Genus, which

Lindheimer has collected beautifully, and I hope that he can be made to go again, if it is wanted. I am much pleased to find a number of your plants of Texas in his collection, e.g. fine specimens of [illegible], [illegible] umbellatum, [illegible] [illegible] [illegible] villosa, [illegible] flexilis, etc.

My leisure time is [illegible] principally [illegible] to [illegible] now that most all my botanical labors are confined to the Nicollet and partial examination of the Texas and Santa Fe plants, which got into my hands. But I must soon finish my examination of the Cuscutae, and will continue to study Cactaceae, &c. after all that my time for more is left me, and shall be very happy to avail myself of your kind offer to communicate specimens from your Herbarium for examination.

And now, before closing permit me to ask you when you will, or can, do something to further your American Flora? This question, I have no doubt, has been put to you and Dr Gray so often by all lovers of botany in this country and by many elsewhere, that you must have [illegible] tired of it! But still the necessity for it is every day felt more deeply.

Very sincerely
yours
George Engelmann

Prof John Torrey

New York

[illegible] [illegible] 22 1848

My dear Doctor

Since I [illegible] with you I had the pleasure to address a few lines to you, especially about the [illegible] Dr. Wislizenus' Report. I have since learned with delight that you gave my paper a hasty examination; [illegible] you had more thoroughly used your critical judgement about it. I have since got Col. Emory's figures of Cacti and they are very unsatisfactory for [illegible] examination; I have however attempted something like a description.

My wish at present is to interest you in Dr. Josiah Gregg's undertaking, who is at this moment at Saltillo and who as you know is an old traveller in Northern Mexico, and who has lately taken up the study of natural history and especially botany with a great deal of zeal and will undoubtedly make valuable observations and collections in those interesting and little known countries. Dr. Gregg desires the war department to afford him the same facilities as were afforded to Fendler and were tendered to Lindheimer, namely a free transportation of his baggage, collections, instruments etc., especially of the collections, which can be done very easily, as they would most always go with return trains which are empty for the greater part. It would enable Dr. Gregg to collect more largely, the advantage of which I need not explain to you. Your movements may soon put a stop to the marches of military forces in Mexico. But as long as our troops are there, the science may as well profit by them.

Does Dr. Wislizenus pay any attention to Cacti & which he could improve his opportunities by directing his observations to their growth, flowering, fructification etc.

Lindheimer has again sent a collection of interesting plants from Northwestern Texas, the granitic region of the upper Colorado. It is remarkable that a number of his plants are identical with New Mexican species and recede more and more from the vegetation of the gulf coast. He has also sent two Cacti, which I consider new, which I at least had not seen before, an Opuntia and another "Echinocereus."

I remain, dear Sir, very truly

yours

Geo. Engelmann

Prof John Torrey

Princeton

N Jersey

My dear Sir

your agreeable lines of March 18th reached me yesterday. You don't know, whether you wrote to me or not lately. Your last letter to me is dated Jan 3d. I wrote to you Jan 19th in answer and again about 8 days ago in behalf of Dr Gregg, who desires from the government facilities of travelling and transportation. As you have seen his collections and know with what [illegible] he hunts up every thing he thinks interesting, you [illegible] try to interest those, who have particularly on your [illegible] granted similar favors to Fendler. — Dr Greggs next collections will be better yet, as he now knows better how to collect. I keep up a correspondence with him and have tried to instruct him as much as possible. He will also number his next collection so that we may understand one another and he us, when we speak of this or that of his plants.

Col Emory wrote me that he had collected fragments of most of the Cactaceae, figured by Stanley, and that they were sent to you. ~~As they~~ If they should still be in your hands you would oblige me very much if you could send them to me, so that I could complete as much as the material will permit my notes on his Cactaceae. He has sent me on your intercession his drawings, you know. They are beautifully executed but entirely without botanical accuracy or botanical detail, so that it is sometimes even uncertain to say to which genus the plant in question belongs. I have tried my best to do something with it, and have ventured to describe them as well as possible. Some I have recognized as old friends; one, with fruit, a true Cereus (I have hardly a doubt ~~but~~ that it is C. greggii Wisl. Report) but such a strange shaped fruit that I am inclined to doubt almost the painter! — a stipitate oval long acuminate fruit! — — The figure of the large Cereus from California I did not get but fortunately had a few seeds which convinced me to recognize it as a true Cereus. — If I could get a few fragments of the plants only, a bunch of spines or so etc etc, I could give a much better account of these plants. I have instructed Col. Emory how to observe the Cacti and I have no doubt he will pay more attention to their characters in future — though the species he may meet between Vera Cruz and Mexico are not so interesting to us as those of the regions bordering on our confines.

Dr Wislizenus was detained in the printing of his report most miserably, but will probably be done with it before the ~~end of~~ middle of this month — so he writes me. Your notes and suggestions in regard to my appendix are very thankfully acknowledged by me and I hope you will always freely tell me if any mistakes I may have made or suggest any alterations you may think proper. —

I have my great doubts about Wislizenia, and am afraid that it must be referred to your Oxystylis as a second species. — You don't mention a stipes of the fruit in Oxystylis, but even if there be none, that alone could possibly not distinguish both plants generically. —

I will have extra copies of my appendix to Dr W's report sent to all my botanical correspondents in this country and Europe.

I shall be glad to see Fremont here. I hope to get some of his duplicates, after they have passed through your hands. — If there is any thing of Cactaceae and Cuscutae in it, which he promised me to collect with particular care, I should offer you to take hold of them and describe them for your work on Fremont's plants — for a work it will become!

I have before me Hooker's plate of Vesicaria Geyeri. It is totally different from my Bilobium. But Bilobium stands to Harvey's Californian Species very nearly as Dithyrea in Hook Jour. Bot.

[illegible] does to Oxystylis! — is it too late that I have
written to Mr. Nt. if it is yet time to alter it in printing,
and mention it as a second species of Dithyrea? — Is your
Morisonia actually D. Gayeri? I thought it must be
my Dithyrea! which is very near Biscutella and not
Vesicaria. — At first glance the shape of the flat
silicle and the short style with the large capitate
stigma distinguish it — one horizontal seed etc.

Where does Nuttall [illegible] his N. Mexican and [illegible]
plants? I should [illegible] a copy if possible.
— And what are the [illegible] works where the
plants of northern Mexico are published? I ask
in reference to Gregg's and Wislizenus' plants.
I have mentioned only a few of them as you know
— principally from fear of collision with others. —
I should like to learn your opinion about my
6 new pines — are they really new? —— The analogy
of the 5 leaved pine of ~~Chihuahua~~ N. Mexico (your P. flexilis)
and that of Chihuahua (P. strobiformis Wisl.) with
P. Strobus is very interesting, but they are very distinct.

Your proposition in relation to the Exploring Expedition
plants is very flattering but after mature consideration
I am obliged to decline it. If I followed my
inclinations I would accept at once, but my
botanical knowledge is so imperfect ~~slight~~ that I would have to
study a good deal ~~[illegible]~~ only to begin to be
able to do justice to the work, I would further
have to give up at least to a great extent
my medical practice which now occupies my
time almost entirely, and just begins to become
lucrative. And then the necessary trip to
Europe would destroy it entirely. — But still I
should like it so well! I feel as much
as I did when my old friend Nicollet 1838
proposed to me to accompany him on his northwestern tour.

You ask, what is to be done with Gregg's plants? Would it not be best to put all those collections together which have been made in Mexico during the war and which can be obtained, Gregg's, Wislizenus', [illegible] etc. and distribute them, as those of the Exploring Expedition are to be distributed for description? — I did not know though whether that would be feasible and whether it could be done well without comparing European herbaria where so much of the Mexican Flora is to be found. — It would add a very good chapter to our „Conquests in Mexico"!

I receive Hooker's Journal irregularly and very late, and am astonished that Seemann collected so few new things.

I remain dear Sir, very truly

yours

G. Engelmann

Prof. J. Torrey

Princeton NJ

My dear Doctor

Last night Dr Halsted delivered your welcome parcel and letter, and requests me to make every thing ready by this morning. The package is done, but not as rich as I wished it to be. You will find however a few plants there, that may interest you. I have also selected all the plants of the balance of [illegible], in my hands, which I thought might interest you — in the printed catalog you will find names, dates etc; I have them not at hand at present.

You will oblige me, my dear Doctor, by sending the included package to Dr Gray and the little paper to Mr Durand.

The label of Oxystylis was there but not the plant! — You will find among mine a fragment of Wislizenia.

Excuse haste and abruptness; I am in great hurry

Very truly

yours

G Engelmann

St Louis Aug 7th 1849

My dear Sir

some months ago I received the fine collection of California plants, of Fremonts Collection you had sent me through Dr Halsted. My intention was to examine them soon or at least those, belonging to families with which I had made myself familiar. Some fine Euphorbiae were among them and others particularly interesting to me.

The Catalogue which you find in this letter was made out, and it was my intention to send it as soon as I could say something more definite about the plants. But that time never came as yet! At first I was very busy in distributing Lindheimers plants, and before I could finish them, the Cholera was upon us, and since then I had to say good bye to botany.

That terrible disease which more than decimated the inhabitants of St Louis kept me for three months almost constantly at work, and I often wonder how I remained so well under that continued and almost incredible physical and mental labor, under all the fatigues and exertions —

I only yesterday began again to write to my friends and correspondents, and I must beg all as I do you ~~not~~ to take offence at my long apparent neglect. — I have to day only time to say that I am living and well and hope to resume my botanical labors with increased zeal, as leisure is granted.

I have received an interesting collection made by Dr Gregg from the Rio Grande to Saltillo & Mexico City. He is gone to California since May last. — There are a number of duplicates a set of which I hope will prove acceptable to you They shall be put out as soon as I have leisure. —

Fendler had gone toward the Salt Lake, but meeting with misfortune, Crossing [illegible] all by flood, he has just returned.

Among Greggs plants is one which may prove the Armoracia — I shall see.

Very truly
my dear Doctor

Yours

Prof J. Torrey
New York

G Engelmann

I enclose an attempt to distinguish 3 Clematis I see one with [illegible] among Greggs, don't know yet whether it will help to unite or distinguish the two mexican forms.

Prof J. Torrey

Princeton

New Jersey

My Dear Sir

your welcome and interesting letter of Sept 13 has been in my hands about 10 days and would have been answered sooner, if Dr Gray had not urged me to send my manuscript on some of Fendlers plants, which I had to finish first.

Together with Fendlers I have studied Wislizenus', Gregg's and Lindheimer's Asclepiadeae, and I believe have trespassed on your grounds a little in that. I find many new species amongst them, and partly of genera not yet represented in the Flora of the U. States — as Roulinia, Metastelma, Sarcostemma; also a number of new Asclepiades; Wislizenus has collected a fine specimen of your A. speciosa, and several new ones and so has Fendler. — Have you examined Gregg's? Among his I find a new Asclepias from Saltillo, which has also been collected by Wislizenus about Paso and Chihuahua, and a new Sarcostemma also coll. by W. about Chihuahua; he has also collected at Ojito April 4th an Anantherix, which I have received from all the collectors, very different from A. paniculata; Lindheimer has sent a 3d species of this genus, which I propose to reestablish; it must not be confounded with Acerates, as Decaisne does. — Fendler and Wisl. have both collected a pretty Asclepias with terminal sessile umbells, which have a sort of involucrum! I shall send in a few days full descriptions to Dr Gray and ask him to submit them to your criticism.

I am also working at the Euphorbiae of those regions. I have now 26 different forms (I will not yet say species) of Euphorbiae stipulatae, most of them west. Fendler has sent a good many of them, Lindheimer some, Wislizenus overlooked them. But Gregg has done finely, under the name of Golondrina, a sort of Milkweed, he has sometimes under one label sent several fine species — some smooth & glaucous, others hairy, each at „Golondrina Valley near Chihuahua 28 & 29 April 47; the same in low collected Valley of the Nazas, 15 April mixed with others, — I named E. stipulacea, with the stipules very conspicuous; seeds smooth. A very similar one is E. Greggii also on the Nazas, 15 April, with favulose rugose seeds, — and mixed with it was one common E. herniarioides! — A very pretty crescent species is from Monterey, coll. in February, which you probably have not yet, and another was mixed with some other plants collected at Cienaga 27 May — somewhat near E. mucronata (your expression — is it certain, that that is Lam.'s mucronata?) but with triangular leaves, and perennial; seeds also somewhat different. — The umbellate Euphorb. sent by Gregg from different places is perhaps not different from E. [illegible] sent from [illegible] Lindh. — Another almost leafless curious species sent from many places has also been obtained by Wislizenus. It is near [illegible]phora, but distinct with tuberous roots etc, I believe undescribed. —

My best thanks for the trouble you have taken in copying Zuccarini's Cowania purpurea. I can not doubt that it is the plant in question, of which you must also have specimens, but I have examined it again and repeat that the calyx is very distinctly and considerably imbricate. — I find that Zuccarini has described many plants from Northern Mexico — where has he obtained them and where are they described. Besides the Krameria, this Cowania, the Dasylirion there may be others of Gregg's & Wisl.' plants described by him. —

I should like to see a flower of your G. Fremontii, it may yet be different from my G. pentagynum; at least Fendler has sent a plant, named by Gray G. pentagynum, but which I find very different.

G. pentagynum: erectum, pedicellis deflexis erectis, glanduloso-pubescentibus; filamentis stylis ima parte solum connatis, inaequalibus, rostro glanduloso-pubescente.

G. (Fendler's) diffusum, pedunculis elongatis, pedicellis deflexis declinatis, [illegible] pubescentibus; filamentis calycem et stylos tertia parte connatos superantibus, rostro puberulo.

My idea certainly was to write a joint article on western pines; I could not do it alone, as I have no knowledge of the eastern pines, nor of all that has been done by others, to attempt it, but I will do what I can to assist you, and do all the labor, which you think proper to charge me with; I may also attempt the drawings, but will not promise much before I have tried.

I have not the least objection to give up the Sapotaceae for the „Amargosa" — but what do you make of it? There appear to be so many anomalous things in those chaparals! — The yellow flowered shrub from San Lorenzo May 11 is also quite unknown to me.

I have written to Col. Emory that you intended sending me his Cactaceae — he thought he had better see them again and rake up his memory for more Data. I doubt whether that would be of much use

Fremont was here last week, and went west. I have written for him a full instruction about many things especially Cactaceae, what to examine and inquire into, how to figure and collect. If you think it would be useful I can send a Copy to Emory and Halsted.

Gregg's Cactaceae — at least my specimens are difficult to name or describe as he collects the flowers only and that, very poorly. As you know many Cactaceae are only known without flowers and almost all can be distinguished without it; but the reverse is not the case — at least has never been attempted. I shall be glad however to see and examine your specimens, and name them if I can.—

Speaking of Euphorbiae — could I see your Euphorbiae? at least the Stipulatae? — is not what you supposed to be E. petaloidea according the same plant, which I named E. Geyeri in Plant. Lindh. — common in all collections from the upper Arkansas, Santa Fe etc, distinguished by the large petaloid appendages? But what then is Pursh's plant of that name from Pennsylvania "pedunculis foliis aequantibus"? — Fendler's plants are specimens of the curious E. hexagona Nutt.

I can find no specimen of the A[illegible] among my set of Gregg's plants. — But in looking over Gregg's & Wislizenus plants to find it, I hit upon two plants, which I had put aside not knowing at the moment where to place them, and found them to be two smooth & glaucous species of Jatropha as now defined; the one from El Paso, the other from the lower Rio grande, both apparently undescribed.—

If you send me any Pines, don't forget to send the cones along.— Please to let Dr Gray know that you are sending me a package, he will add several things.—

As regards Pines or Coniferae in general I repeat that I shall with pleasure undertake any part you would assign to me; but I have never studied them yet! Never examined a Pine I believe, before the new species of Wislizenus forced me to do it.— The second consideration is my time! If it must be done soon — I can not undertake it as all my leisure time will be already occupied for some time to come.— You must do as you think best. —

The best, though not cheapest way would be by Adams Express, which connects with Greens Express, who have an Agency here — I have several times sent to Dr Gray boxes or packages by that line. — If you know of a cheaper and as safe way, I would of course prefer it.

What do you say about Sagittariae? It is unfortunately so difficult to obtain the ripe fruit, and that appears to me to be of such great importance in determining the identity or difference of species. I have now been enabled to compare ripe fruit of the European S. sagittif. and find it certainly very distinct from ours. — The stamens offer also an unlooked for character. In some species they are subulate and smooth in others shorter, more or less conic and glandulous. — I am so far certain only of 5 species in the U. States, but my collection is limited and there may be many which I have not yet got. It appears difficult too to identify the species of the different Authors. [illegible] Is S. simplex actually always dioicous? Then it can not be the plant I have always taken for it.

The Sagittariae offer a fine field, but I am afraid they can not be studied satisfactorily but in the field in the fresh specimens and a large number so as to observe all forms and variations.

I remain Very truly, my dear Sir

yours

Prof. J. Torrey
Princeton NJ

G. Engelmann

Can you satisfactorily distinguish Quercus tinctoria and Q. coccinea? These both trees appear to have so many intermediate forms, which defy the attempt to class them

You will have wondered what has become of me — but probably our friend Gray has informed you that I am still here! With the exception of about 2 weeks strolling about the country I have been steady at work; but I am a very slow worker, and have only this week finished my Cacti, and have now begun with Euphorbia, in which your collection kindly sent some time ago has ~~materially~~ vastly increased the material to be worked up. I find it a greater labor than I had anticipated, and more ~~doubts~~ arising than

I thought, in agony when the characters are so striking — just the reverse of the everlasting sameness and uniformity but greatest vacillation of the Cactaceae, especially the Opuntiae:—

I had hoped and expected to be in New York before the end of last month — but am determined now to work it out — even if my departure to Europe should fall in November or even later, — but I have given up to work out Asclepiadaceae before I leave, for which I have brought good Materials with me.—

Among your plants was a parcel, labelled "to be sent to Dr Engelmann", plants in dark grey paper; ~~as~~ are these as a present or as a loan?

You note that you have described my Euph. Wislizeni in Thurbers collection — where published? or not yet published? and what is your name? and where do I find a note of Euphorbia published by you some time ago?
I believe E. Wislizeni has been published by Bentham as E. radians some time

in New York and of spending a few days with you; but when it will be, I have no means of calculating yet. —

Very faithfully

yours

G. Engelmann

When I arrived here in December last I immediately enquired about your engravings and drawings and wrote to you about their state of forwardness. Have you ever got that letter? I doubt it as Gray did not get his, sent about the same time. Since a few weeks I am again in Paris and learn that Mlle Taillant has finished all the engravings she had in hand — and that the plates have been forwarded to you. Prof Decaisne says that he despairs ever hearing from you again as you never acknowledged the receipt of the former batch sent to you, and which I saw in New York at the printers. Please write to him if you should not have done so already. ~~He~~ says he has not heard from you since years.

And how have my Cactaceae of the Railroad expedition gone on? How did that lithographer in New York

Could you not send me a copy of the plates, and of the text too if printed -? I am very anxious to see both; — and must say I am a little fearful about both. My hope for the text is in Gray who will have seen and corrected it, and for the plates in you.

I have not heard how they progress with my Boundary Cactaceae in Washington. Here I find it pretty difficult to get along fast enough. I have only about 14 plates finished, and 12 more are in the hands of engravers while 10 remain as yet in my hands. They are done in first rate style, and will please you and Col Emory. How is he progressing with the rest of the Boundary Report, Natural history and all?

Mrs Engelmann sends her love to your ladies, and so do I.

Will you write me? Can you find time for it? How are Asclepiadeae? — I continue busy with Cuscuteae and also with Euphorbiae about both of which I have written to Gray.

Ever truly yours

G. Engelmann

My Dear Doctor

Excuse pen and ink—
I am a traveller and can not
give it better than I have it!
Thank you for your kind letter
and ready answer — certainly
unlooked for.

Last Sunday I spent with Mr
Scheer at Northfleet — nothing
very profitable for Cactaceae there
— but there and I believe at Hookers
also I for the first time saw
a part of the ~~Bounding~~ Cactus
by Rebut, (which you might have
send me direct—!) they, on the whole
pleased me much, some things I
would have altered, if I had had
a proof; but with Akermann's (?)
work I am not satisfied at all
this Echin. Whipplei is as pale
as death, why you can hardly see
what it is — the engraver seems
to have been afraid to make a
black line or dot! —

for those Colum publications; also for 2 or 3 copies of Bristeles Coates plates. — I want 200 copies of them with the text. Is that printed? I have seen the Manuscript in the printers hands in Washington last November and corrected it some — but want you or Gray to do so more, if not printed yet — it wants revision badly. Write to Bigelow if you please —

Please send me the few copies of Ail R. Coates soon. Frankfurt on the Main, Germany, is always my direction for 5 or 6 months to come yet. —

Since I wrote you I have seen Roemer; he says he sent you 60 odd ~~plates~~ drawings and has some dozen more to do, which will not be finished before end of the year. but the plates have been sent long ago — Emory writes me about them — but I got his letter only here as young if I had had them in Paris I could have done something, or enquired about those things — there seems to be a general misunderstanding. — my respects to your Ladies

ever truly yours G. Engelmann

It was very stupid in me not to have answered your kind and early communications. I might have told you to forward the package to Gray who was sending me a whole lot of things. These have come now, and the opportunity is thus lost.

I have also neglected to write to Mr Thurber and to Mr Buckley.

But some little excuse should be found in my present distracted state. I have moved to my house only a week ago, and am in the midst of every kind of confusion; while for the first six weeks of my stay here I have been moving about from Hotels to Boarding houses and back, have been smoked burned and washed out (without, happily, loosing much) and have been in constant contact and therefore trouble with mechanics repairing and refitting my house — and I am not through with it yet.

Tell Mr Thurber that I have collected the Aristida in abundance, but not met with the Eragrostis. My first business, when my herbarium is in a little order (It is boxed up yet.) will be to send him the Grasses.

Prof Gray sent me the other day a note of Dr Darlington about the tubers of Sagittaria variabilis borne at the end of stolons, and from the size of a pea to that of an egg. I have seen them also as large as filberts; S. graminea (simplex) bears them also. But another question here obtrudes itself. Is this not the case with all the perennial Sagittariae and are there not some Sagittariae annual? Is S. pusilla and my S. calycina of which I gave you a specimen 2 years ago annual? This latter I have found again this fall but the ~~ground~~ high waters in the summer, which also injured Nymphaea and Nelumbium seem to have prevented the plant from growing (or germinating?) till late in summer; all the plants that I could find — and there were hundreds of them, — were small, most of them with lanceolate leaves or with phyllodia only, and with few, often only with single flowers!

I had proposed to myself to do a great deal before I would get involved in the practice of my profession — but I have not found time for any thing and at the same time my professional ~~labours~~ services are already frequently required. —

I shall send my Grossularia to Mr Thurber and when he returns them you will perhaps have the kindness to send me the package along with them.

I shall be much obliged to you for some copies of your boundary report, and if you would permit me to pay for them I would take half a dozen.

Dr Newberry promised to send me his Euphorbiae Cucurbitae Cactaceae etc.

If Thurber will do the Grapes he has a deal of work before him! my respects to him

Ever yours

G. Engelmann

Dear Sir

permit me to introduce to your acquaintance my brother Henry Engelmann, who on his way to Washington is passing through your city.

Though no botanist my brother has done a good deal in collecting plants on his expeditions to the Rocky Mountains and Utah, and as I believe I have told you before, was the main cause of the discovery of

the true nature of the Buffalo grass. He also brought living specimens of both sexes and of the Bouteloua oligostachya, which now flourish with me.

My Brother is chemist and assayer, and would be much pleased if you would permit him an insight into your assay office in Wallstreet.

I am still at Euphorbiae. Boissier, who is doing them for the Prodromus, has several new species of our Flora.

Very respectfully and truly

Though our correspondence has been carried on very negligently and has stopped, I believe for a couple of years — as if years were as days only — I very often had the good intention to write and to tell you how we have come on here and how we have gradually become naturalized again in Missouri, and so much so that we feel and hope with four fifths of our Missourians for a speedy termination of this terrible war. But no more of this now.

I am led to write you just now on account of the nice botanical collection brought home by Dr Parry an (incomplete) set of which he has communicated to me.

Among other things he has sent home Pines; as also my Brother of the species.

This little group of Nut pines requires revision. My brother has brought your P. monophyllos from the mountains about Salt Lake. I think it is different from P. edulis; but as at present informed, I am inclined to the believe that your P. Llaveana is not Schiede's plant which has 3 leaves in a sheath; nor is Dr Newberry correct in referring his pine to P. cembroides.

I guess — and it is mere guess-work so far — that they might be arranged thus:

1. Pinus monophyllos Torr & Frem 1 leaf
2 P. edulis Eng 2 leaves
3. P. cembroides Zucc. 3 leaves
Syn. P. Llaveana Schied
P. osteosperma Eng.
4. P. Parryi (P. Llaveana Torr non Schiede) 5 leaves.

P. Llaveana & P. cembroides, are described in the original work with usually 3 leaves!

the cones of those 4 pines are difficult if not impossible to distinguish — but I believe it ~~not~~ probable that the number of leaves should vary so much in a <u>single</u> species, — if, however, no other good characters should be found, we would have to unite all four of them, hard as it may seem!

As to Newberry's P. cembroides I have a notion that it is nothing but a stunted alpine form of what I have taken all along for P. flexilis, though among the numerous forms, brought home by all travellers, I have seen no such small cones; the scales however and the nuts are not different. —

But the question arises whether what Nuttall and I have all along taken for P. flexilis is not something else? and I wish you would, as you no doubt are able to, decide and solve my doubts — which Newberry seems to share; you say "cones erect" and you compare the scales with those of P. rigida! — While my flexilis is said to have pendulous cones which can not at all compared with P. rigida but the branches are certainly flexible. I do not have James' work — and can not compare his description.

Have Lewis & Clark's pines named by Rafinesque, ever been identified?

Dr Parry has collected another very pretty, and I believe new, alpine Pine, which I think would properly be named P. aristata, the mucro of the scales terminating in a long and conspicuous awn! which gives the cone a very peculiar appearance but at last disappears (in old specimens). Leaves, all 5s, very resinous; cones short, petiolous or erect; seeds small with large wings or else I would take it for James' P. flexilis; It must be the Pine mentioned by you in Fremont Report p. 97. and Gunnison's Report p. 130. I can not identify it with any other described Pine nor does it seem assimilate to any of ours so far as I can see.

Could you let me have a single leaf or bunch of leaves of your Fremont's Pine and Gunnison's and James' original flexilis? — If you could, I would be much obliged to you. — Also your P. Llaveana

Parry says that Pinus flexilis does not reach the highest elevations while Pinus aristata is confined to the alpine summits and is often quite prostrate; just as Newberry describes his P. cembroides."

this close analogy or rather connection of those 4 nutpines shows that the division of Pines into sections, partially or wholly characterized by the number of leaves, is untenable, and it reminds me of the division of Cactaceae after the form of their spines, or external appearance, while a better knowledge of their organs of fructification leads to a very different classification. Thus the globose Echinocactus Williamsii is no doubt an Anhalonium, etc etc. — My brother had brought some nice Cactaceae from Utah, several of them very striking new forms; I had figured and described them but they have other things to do at Washington but to print scientific Reports!

In his report I have also reëxamined Ephedra and think that I have a Nevada species distinct from E. antisyphilitica and I consider your species, indicated by you in Emory's Report as well distinguished; I have the same in structurally morphologically and systematically, but the opportunities are comparatively small here. Besides that, you will be astonished to learn it, I have fallen upon the mucors and mildews and exceedingly regret the impossibility to communicate with our friend Curtis, who could enlighten me on many points.

You know that that Sagittaria calycina has also been found in Maine in Delaware, and now in northern Illinois, so it is probably diffused all over the country, but has been overlooked.

Dr Newberry who was here a few weeks ago informs me that you have the Smithsonian Collections in your hands, and he promised to see that I should get a set of the Spec. of Pines especially the Cones. --

Ever truly yours
G. Engelmann

My dear Doctor

You see, I am not to be put off by silence. Here I am again.

Those nutpines trouble me a great deal, and I should like to clear up some of the difficulties or all, if possible.

About the same time I wrote to you, I also addressed a letter to Prof Braun of Berlin, and he had the kindness to send me a few branches of leaves of the original P. Llaveana and also of P. cembrodes (though not the original. I shall get from Dr Parry his specimen of your Llaveana, But to conclude I must have a few leaves or a branch of Newberry's P. cembrodes to compare. Would you have the

kindness to send me in a letter
a fragment, however small?

Have you got specimens of
what we take for 'Jamesii' and
your P. flexilis? I still think
that Newberry's plant must be
an alpine form of the same.
I have got cones and specimens
of several collectors and can let
you have some, if agreeable
to you.

I have among Parry's and
other plants a batch a new
Gentianes, and one of them
(of not the new ones!) is your
G. Fremontiana and not
different from the Siberian
G. humilis, which the description
in De Candolle would leave in
doubt, but my ~~Siberian~~
Siberian specimens prove
to be so without any doubt.

Is Mr Thurber in New York
and what is he doing?
Is he going along with his

Work on Western Botany ?

You had the kindness many years ago to send me specimens of Bernardi's collections, numbered or lettered. Have you named them anywhere, and how could I obtain your names. The Oaks would interest me now especially.

My intention was last year to visit New York Philadelphia and Cambridge to study my brothers Utah plants etc, but times prevented me and I do not know now when I shall get there — financially nothing lately is in a most miserable state with us.

Ever truly

Yours,

G Engelmann

www.ingramcontent.com/pod-product-compliance
Lightning Source LLC
Chambersburg PA
CBHW020235090426
42735CB00010B/1699
* 9 7 8 3 3 3 7 3 2 1 1 1 6 *